Tales of Old Essex

Tales of
Old Essex

Adrian Gray

With Illustrations by Don Osmond

COUNTRYSIDE BOOKS

NEWBURY, BERKSHIRE

First Published 1987
Reprinted 1992
© Adrian Gray 1987

COUNTRYSIDE BOOKS
3 CATHERINE ROAD
NEWBURY, BERKSHIRE

ISBN 0 905392 98 1

Produced through MRM Associates Ltd, Reading
Typeset by Acorn Bookwork, Salisbury
Printed in England by J. W. Arrowsmith Ltd., Bristol

To Jean, Viv and Ros –
for services to history in Essex

Contents

CONTENTS

ESSEX – The map overleaf is by John Speede and shows the county as it was in the early seventeenth century.

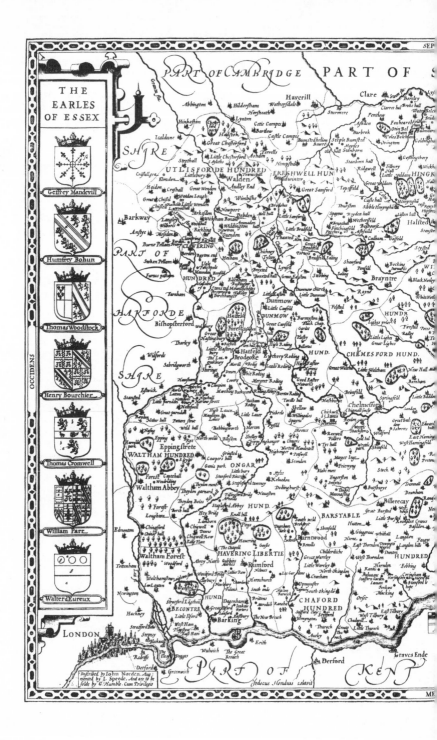

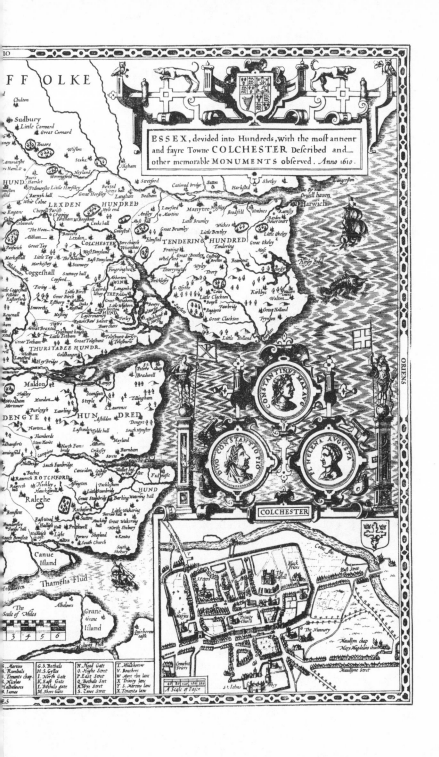

The Dunmow Flitch

MOST legends tend to change as they are passed down through the generations, and few people today can even hazard a guess at the origins of the curious Dunmow Flitch ceremony in which couples who have lived happily through a year of marriage are awarded a flitch of bacon. Different people have had varying ideas as to what started it all, and in 1877 one Essex labourer summed it up in a true earthy style – 'Them ancient foaks – maybe the Rumans – guv' a bit o' bacon to them as didn't whop their missus.'

Another tradition dates the origins of the ceremony back to the Middle Ages and Sir Reginald Fitzwalter. Sir Reginald and his wife had enjoyed a year of blissful married life and decided to get their union blessed by the Prior of Little Dunmow. However, they decided to dress up as a poor couple and in this guise they begged a blessing from the Prior. He was so impressed by their devotion to each other that he asked the priory cook to give them a flitch (or whole side) of bacon. Sir Reginald promptly revealed his true identity and gave some land to the Priory on the condition that a flitch was presented to any other couple prepared to swear that they had passed through a year of marriage without ever having second thoughts.

The ceremony was certainly established by the 1400s because a flitch was won by Richard Wright in 1445. In fact he was the only person known to have got a real flitch, all others being awarded merely a gammon or thigh.

At least two other men are known to have successfully sworn of their happiness before the Prior, who was of course done away with at the Dissolution of the Monasteries by Henry VIII.

The ceremony recommenced in 1701 under the guidance of the Lord of the Manor of Little Dunmow. Two couples were 'tried' before a 'jury' of five maidens, four of whom were daughters of the Lord of the Manor. A Wethersfield couple named Shakeshaft were 'tried' before six bachelors and six spinsters in 1751, being awarded a flitch to the cheers of 5,000 onlookers. Mrs Shakeshaft said that she had only one regret in her married life – that she hadn't got married sooner! The Shakeshafts were able to make £50 by selling off portions of their bacon.

After this the ceremony again fell out of fashion, due largely to uninterested Lords. When John Gilder and his wife from Terling tried to claim a flitch in 1772 they arrived to find the Priory gates locked fast. A Reading cheesemonger was also spurned in 1832, although this may have been partially due to his complicated romantic history. The man's name was Vines, and he was successful in his business until his wife died. She was apparently a 'fascinating and witty woman in affluent circumstances', but after her death he decided to retire. However, retirement did not suit Vines as he soon became lonely, missing 'the rattle of scales and the chatter of customers'.

To provide solace in his autumn years, the cheesemonger sought a new wife, though uncharitable commentators said that his interest in a woman depended chiefly on her personal wealth. His own attractions must have been limited, since he was apparently a heavy drinker and something of a miser. Nonetheless he soon found a woman with wealthy relations who seemed like a good match and a family party was arranged to introduce him to the bride's side. At the end of the meal several glasses were left on the table by guests who had drunk as much beer as they could manage; this conspicuous waste was too much for Vines's sensibilities, and he emptied all the dregs into his own glass, quaffing the lot in one go. His only comment was, 'It's a pity such good things should be wasted.'

This exhibition of bad manners brought that romance to an end, but within three weeks he had met a farmer's widow and was paying court to her instead! This lady, Mrs Stevens, had once kept a boarding school and it was reckoned that Vines considered she must have some worthwhile savings stored away somewhere. He soon married her and, on account of getting through married life for a year and a day without harsh words, claimed the flitch.

The refusal of the flitch, and the Lord's evident lack of interest in the ceremony, nearly resulted in the whole process being hi-jacked by the town of Saffron Walden. Little Dunmow was all too content to let it die.

When the flitch was eventually hi-jacked it didn't get taken too far – just a few miles up the road to Great Dunmow. In 1855 a Flitch Committee was formed that broke the link with Little Dunmow Priory, but at least it put some energy into the proceedings. Some people felt that it was merely an attempt to publicise the town in connection with a local railway proposal. However, a jury of six men and six women was appointed and five shillings was charged for a seat in the Town Hall during the 'trial'. Two couples were selected from many applicants, and both were awarded flitches. A procession was then made to Windmill Field where 7,000 had gathered.

After that, trials were held sporadically every few years. Some people considered the whole thing rather vulgar, and in 1877 claimant John Haltridge went home in disgust after he found he was expected to answer some rather personal questions!

The 1880 ceremony was said to have a rather low social tone. The 'Judge' was apparently deaf and both the claimants wore large gold ear-rings. A lot of drinking took place so that in future years the Police gathered to check excesses; the whole thing was dampened down by a thunderstorm.

In 1885 Lord Northwick, aged 74, gained a flitch after a private correspondence with the Lord of the Manor. He was said to be so proud of it that he had it pickled so that it could be kept as a family heirloom. A couple were refused a flitch in 1899 as the jury considered 'that there was an absence of love when there was an empty stomach'. Perhaps they should have made a humanitarian gesture and awarded the flitch *because* of this!

The modern age was entered in 1901 with commercial sponsorship by Bovril and in 1912 the prizes were given by the Dunmow Flitch Bacon Company. Despite interruptions by two world wars and attempts by other towns like Ilford to start their own flitch traditions, Dunmow has retained its fame for the curious ceremony of awarding pieces of bacon to loving couples.

How Hornchurch got its Name

How did Hornchurch get its name? Many say it has something to do with the carved head of an ox or bull that had been displayed on the eastern gable of St Andrew's church for many years. But there are many different legends surrounding the name of Hornchurch.

One legend goes that the name of 'Hornchurch' came from an incident that occurred during the building of the church itself. As the building workers were hard at work, the King was enjoying some hunting in the neighbouring forest and fields. The King's dogs succeeded in killing a hart, the horns of which were put into the wall of the church.

Another legend says that the church was paid for by a female convert to Christianity in repentance for a lifetime of fairly colourful sin. The church thus became known as 'Horechurch' in memory of the woman's previous activities. A passing king took exception to this rather undignified name for a church and decreed that in future it should be known as 'Hornchurch', to fix the memory of which he had some horns put up on the church.

By the year 1384 the Priors of Hornchurch were certainly using the head and horns as a symbol, but it should perhaps be noted that the area was already well-known for its leather and skin trade. Perhaps Hornchurch was built with money from the animal trade, just as the Suffolk churches were sometimes built with money from the wool trade.

15

Eventually control of the Priory passed to New College, Oxford. Every year the College gave a boar's head to be competed for on Christmas Day. This was always cooked at Hornchurch Hall, where the first slice was cut off, and then it was carried through the streets to the field by the church. A pitchfork was traditionally used to carry the head into the field, always with an orange in its mouth. The prize was competed for in wrestling contests, but the tradition was stopped after 1868 as the Victorian middle-classes considered it an encouragement to working class misbehaviour.

There are some other legends about the name Hornchurch. One says that a local man was on his way home late at night and decided to cut across the field by the church. As he did so he was attacked by a wild boar, a powerful and vicious animal. No matter how he fought he couldn't get away, and the man was beginning to despair of his life when a huge bull came bellowing out of the darkness and chased the boar away. The man was just feeling pleased about the timely arrival of the bull when he realised that the beast was now turning its attention to him! For the second time in a few minutes he had to fight for his life and in this case he managed to kill the bull. He was rather sad about this, since the bull had saved him from the boar, and commemorated the bull by having its horns put up on the church. At least this story seems to account for both the bull's horns and the boar's head, and even takes place close to the church.

An alternative version says that the incident in the field involved the Prior who was on his way to the church. Just as he was walking through the grass he was attacked by a bull, but in this case he was saved through the intervention of some cows which surrounded and protected him.

There are many possible explanations for the horned head on Hornchurch church and these are just a few of them. It could be just a symbol of the old priory, some have even suggested that it represents the Roman cult of Mithras-worship – I don't suppose the vicar would be very happy about that!

Dick Turpin

Most of us had our imaginations populated in childhood by some distinctly 'semi-historical' characters. Into this category we can put figures who *may* have existed, but no-one is quite sure about (like King Arthur), and people who *did* exist but whose stories have got rather distorted down the years (like Dracula). A lot of this is the fault of the Victorians, who liked a story to be as sentimental as possible. If an historical character didn't quite match what they wanted, then they were quite prepared to 'revise' him a little.

Like most highwaymen, Dick Turpin has had his image rather romanticised down the years, but there is no doubt that he was an out and out villain. He was not the lovable sort of villain who used to crop up in Ealing Comedy films – Turpin was undoubtedly a nasty and murderous character. He was born in 1705 in the little country village of Hempstead, in the north-western part of Essex. His birthplace was actually a public house called *The Bell*, though it was later renamed *The Crown*. Young Turpin was apprenticed to a butcher and sent off to Whitechapel. Carving up meat seemed a hard way to make his fortune, so Turpin decided to take a few short cuts by stealing some cattle from a farmer in Plaistow and selling them to another butcher.

He then abandoned his apprenticeship and became involved with the blackest of criminal characters. After a spot

of smuggling in the Canvey Island district, he joined a band of vicious robbers called Gregory's Gang. This unpleasant group marauded around the countryside east of London. Their specialities were raiding isolated farmhouses and churches – in one night they visited both Chingford and Barking churches.

The gang had discovered that they could terrorise their victims into giving up some of their household treasures, for the farmhouses were always far from help. However, most victims usually tried to keep something hidden from the robbers (those were the days when only a madman would keep his money in a bank!). The gang's solution to this was to torture their victims until their secret hiding place was revealed. Their favourite technique was to hold the farmer's wife over a blazing fire, causing her to shriek with agony until she told the secret of the treasure store.

Turpin still had time for his more personal romantic activities, and in 1727 he married Hester Palmer from East Ham. He set her up in a cottage at Sewardstone, where he laid low between bouts of thieving.

The Gregory Gang was very active in 1735. They raided a number of properties around London, including the farm-house of a Mr Saunders at Charlton. The robbers coolly knocked on the door in the early evening and, when it was opened, stormed into the house. Their sudden arrival rather spoilt a cards-party in the front parlour but at least Gregory, Turpin and the gang enjoyed the wine and mince-pies that had been laid on for refreshments after the cards. A maid locked herself into her attic room when the raiders entered the house, and she remained there – screaming constantly – while they ransacked the house.

The following week they attacked a house in Croydon, and then another in Edgware. The owner of the latter, a Mr Laurence, had a kettle of water thrown over him and a maid was 'shamefully treated'. There was a public outcry following this attack, and a reward of 100 guineas was offered for the gang. They replied by raiding an old lady's house at Loughton, and they actually burned her over her own fire before making off with £400.

Following this, things got a little 'hot' for Turpin and he was nearly caught whilst drinking in Westminster. Others of the gang were not so lucky, and three were executed before 1735 was over.

After this Turpin seems to have decided that it was safer to work on his own. He was responsible for several robberies in Clerkenwell, Islington and Holloway, coming into London from his hideouts on Hackney Marsh and in Epping Forest. By 1736 he was a fully-fledged highwayman, accosting travellers on the Cambridge and Epping routes as they passed through the Forest.

In February 1736 he stopped a finely-dressed man on horseback with the customary words about taking money or life. Turpin must have been surprised when the man burst out laughing. 'What? Dog eat dog?' the man asked, then revealed himself to be another highwayman named King.

The two men then started operating together. They constructed a cave deep in the Forest near High Easter, to which supplies of food were brought by Mrs Turpin. From there they rode out to rob and terrorise innocent travellers.

It was overconfidence on Turpin's part that led to the capture of King. One day they stole a famous horse called *White Stockings* from a Mr Major. This was an error, since the horse had distinctive markings, and an Epping landlord decided to try and trace it. The trail led him to the *Red Lion* in Whitechapel and, of course, to Turpin and King. In the ensuing scramble, King was captured; Turpin, trying to rescue him, shot and killed him instead.

Turpin himself seems to have had considerable luck in evading capture. In April 1737 he was tracked to his cave by a bounty-hunter named Thomas Morris. Turpin at first thought the man was a poacher, but when he realised the truth he shot the man dead. On another occasion he was said to have been holding up a coach when another approached from the opposite direction; instead of escaping, Turpin coolly held up both coaches at the same time.

However, Essex was clearly becoming too dangerous a place and Turpin moved north.

After a while Turpin got into a row with a member of the local gentry, as a result of which he was arrested. Turpin was taken to a cell in York where he was sentenced to be executed on 7th April 1739. As he made his way to the gallows, Turpin tried to appear the cool and dispassionate highwayman of legend, but as he stood still his nerves betrayed him and his leg began to tremble. Angrily he stamped it down. But it hardly mattered, for within minutes he was dead.

The
Convict
Clergyman

I N 1853 a distinguished Professor of Theology was appointed
Rector of Hadleigh, in southern Essex. When he went to
Hadleigh to find out what the place and its church were like,
he received something of a shock. The parsonage house was a
ruin! Clearly there was no prospect of the distinguished
professor being able to live in it since several locals seemed to
have removed parts of it for use in their own properties, and
what remained had been turned into a storehouse for all sorts
of rubbish. There was nothing to do but to sell off the house –
its condition was so bad that it fetched only £10 – and build a
replacement for the distinguished Professor. Clearly the
Professor had some influential friends, for the new house cost
£1,600 – a lot of money in the 1850s.

But how did Hadleigh parsonage get into this deplorable
state? The man who had previously been Rector of Hadleigh,
from 1825 until 1853, was Rev. John Mavor, but he was
peculiarly unable to attend to his duties in the parish for one
simple reason – he was in prison!

John Mavor was born at Woodstock in Oxfordshire in 1786.
His father was a well-known authority on educational topics
and was the author of a spelling book. Young Mavor obviously followed in his father's footsteps to a certain extent, for

he became a student at Wadham College, Oxford, in 1802 when only sixteen. He left the College in 1806 and then applied for a fellowship at Lincoln College; this fellowship was only open to Oxfordshire people, so Mavor was able to secure it.

Mavor was certainly quite an intelligent man, but he also seems to have been rather insufferable. Immensely satisfied with himself, haughty, and totally lacking in tolerance for others, he soon made a nuisance of himself at Lincoln College. In 1823 the College appointed him Curate of Foresthill; as this was five miles away, the College fellows perhaps hoped they would see less of Mavor in the future.

In 1825 they also appointed him Rector of Hadleigh in Essex, which Lincoln College could easily do since they were Patrons of the living. This meant that they could appoint a clergyman of their choice to look after the parish. Another strange practice at the time was that a clergyman who was appointed to a living didn't always do the work there, but would instead get another (less well-connected) cleric to do the work for him.

This was exactly what Mavor planned to do. He had no desire to tend to the needs of a group of Essex people at all, and so planned to get a curate to do the work in Hadleigh while he stayed at Foresthill. There was not a great deal to do in the Oxfordshire parish, so Mavor planned to develop a sideline in preparing young men for ordination. Accordingly he borrowed a sizable sum of money to rebuild his Oxford-shire parsonage (caring not a jot about the Essex one), and turned it into something altogether more suitable for a man of his ambitions.

But things didn't quite turn out as Mavor had hoped. The few pupils he started with declined to none at all – probably because of the unpleasant side of his character which must have made him a poor teacher of future clergymen. This left him short of money to pay back the loan on the rebuilding of the parsonage.

The sad result of all this was that the Rector of Hadleigh

was taken off to the Debtors' Prison in Oxford Castle, where he was to languish for many long years. It was common in those days for people in debt to be put in prison, and of course once you were inside it was difficult to raise the money to pay off your debts and thus get out again! Most county gaols had a wing devoted to the debtors, who often had a more miserable existence than the criminal convicts.

The men who Mavor owed money to then began trying to squeeze as much out of his assets as they could. He was still – in name, at least, Rector of Hadleigh, and that meant that certain payments from the church there would be coming to him. They therefore hired the meanest cleric they could find to do the work, and pocketed the cash from the burials, marriages etc.

After a few years the income from the Parish of Hadleigh had more than covered Mavor's initial debts, but still the money-lenders kept him in prison. They were on to a good thing, after all! Mavor's colleagues tried to advise him that he could obtain release from gaol if he would only apply for it in the right way, but Mavor was so obstinate that he refused all advice.

To their credit, the College fellows did not abandon him. Many of them visited him regularly and even enjoyed his scholarly conversation. However, if the talk came round to the subject of his debts, Mavor would become inflamed with fury and anger. Nor was he idle whilst in gaol, for he became the unofficial prison chaplain and lectured all the other prisoners on their faults – whilst remaining permanently blind to his own. One curious thing about his position was that the gaol was within the bounds of the University, and Mavor therefore counted as a 'resident fellow'; this meant he could vote in University elections, for which he was escorted out of the gaol to the nearest polling place.

The prison was, of course, a very dirty place and it was hard for a clergyman to maintain a dignified appearance in such a situation. Some of the College fellows therefore clubbed together each year to buy him a new suit. For a number of years they bought him one suit in a black, clerical cloth each year, but this material didn't seem to be very hard-wearing. It was therefore suggested to him that he should have future suits in a more practical cloth, but Mavor refused to have anything but the correct outfit for a clergyman. He was certainly a stubborn character!

In 1847 the Bishop of Oxford had Mavor removed from the Curacy of Foresthill, which annoyed the convict clergyman a great deal. He decided that this was the fault of the man who lived at Foresthill Manor, and swore that vengeance would fall on the man. Six years later this man was passing by the Castle, in which Mavor was imprisoned, when he was struck with apoplexy. When Mavor heard about this he was so excited that he suffered a stroke and died!

This brought to an end the unusual career of the Rector of Hadleigh, a clergyman who saw rather more of the inside of a prison than he did of the inside of his own parish church.

The
Three Heads
of the Well

Essex has some of its own fairy stories or legends, and the story of 'The Three Heads of the Well' is certainly a rather strange little tale. As a story, it is said to be centuries old and that the two main characters in it were actually Old King Coel (*not* 'Cole') and Saint Helena. Whoever they were no-one now knows for certain, but without any doubt it is the sort of story that would have made any child shiver in its bed after having heard it as a bed-time story!

Many hundreds of years ago, long before even King Arthur's time, there was a king who lived in Colchester. He was a good king, being well-known for being strong and valiant. He was said to be good with a joke, but as our story will show he wasn't always very wise in his decisions.

The King ruled happily for many years, managing to defeat his enemies in battle and bring peace to his people. He had one child, a beautiful little princess, but when she was about fifteen years old the Queen died.

For a while the King was very upset, but then he heard tell of a wealthy widow lady. The King of Colchester was a little short of money after the cost of defeating his enemies, and so he decided to marry this widow even though she was 'old, ugly, hook-nosed and hump-backed'. The old widow had a daughter who was very similar to her, being rather dowdy, club-footed and of an envious and evil disposition.

It did not take long before the old widow and her malicious daughter had poisoned the King's mind against the beautiful princess. The King was certainly good at fighting battles, but he was not very good at handling two scheming women. His daughter realised that she would not be happy in Colchester any longer, and so she begged her father's permission to leave and seek her fortune elsewhere.

The King thought about this for a while, but he was eventually persuaded to let the princess go by her ugly step-mother; the stepmother knew that if the princess never returned, her own club-footed daughter would be heir to the kingdom. So the King instructed his wife to prepare some food for the princess, and then he gave her permission to go. The old stepmother gave her a canvas bag, containing a chunk of stale bread, a lump of hard cheese and an old bottle of beer.

The princess set off, not with any real idea as to where she was going but confident in seeking her own fortune. After a while she met an old man, who seemed to be a sort of hermit who lived at the roadside. Now, if this was a modern story the princess would no doubt be warned not to talk to strangers, but being the 'old days' she had no doubts about the old man at all. Instead, she sat down beside him and shared her meagre lunch.

The old man was pleased with her generosity and decided to share his only possession with her – his wisdom. He told her that as she continued her journey she would come to a thick, brambly hedge. If she tried to force her way through it, it would rip her clothes and scratch deeply into her skin. The hedge was almost impossible to pass except with the aid of a magic wand, which the old man gave to the princess. He instructed her to strike the hedge three times with the wand and then call out, 'Pray, hedge, let me come through'. Later on, he said, she would find a well, and if she sat on its edge three golden heads would appear and speak to her. She must be certain to listen to them, he advised.

28

Thanking the old man for his help, the princess set off again. Everything happened exactly as he had told her – the hedge parted to let her through, and then she came to the well. She sat down beside it and soon a golden head floated up out of it. The head spoke to her in a rhyme:

> 'Wash me and comb me
> And lay me down softly,
> And lay me on a bank to dry,
> That I may look pretty
> When someone comes by.'

The princess did exactly as the head had asked her, combing its golden hair with a silver comb. Then she placed it on a primrose bank, and sat down to wonder what was going to happen next. Then a second head appeared from the well, making the same request as the first, after which a third head appeared until she had the three all in a row on the bank.

As the heads lay next to each other, they began to consult. 'What shall we do for this young lady, since she's been so kind to us?' one of the heads asked its colleagues. They muttered together, and then they told the princess what they had decided.

The first head announced that it would increase the girl's beauty so much that she would be able to enchant even the most powerful prince in the land. The second head promised that both her body and her breath would be so sweetly perfumed that even the flowers would not be able to compete with her. The third head promised her the good fortune to become queen to the greatest prince. Then they asked her to put them down the well again, and of course she did so as carefully as possible.

Soon after this a young king was out hunting with his nobles when he caught sight of the beautiful young lady, though he didn't know she was a princess. The princess was shy and tried to hide from him, but her delicate aroma gave her presence away and the King soon found her. Of course they fell in love immediately, and she was taken back to the young King's palace where he asked permission to marry her. As they got to know each other better, the princess told her lover that she was the King of Colchester's daughter, and so the young King decided to visit her father.

His arrival in Colchester caused consternation in the royal household. The King of Colchester was delighted at how happily things had turned out for his daughter; no doubt he felt a little guilty too. But his ugly queen and her club-footed daughter were filled with malice.

The old Queen decided that her daughter, too, must leave and seek her fortune. So she packed a bag full of sweetmeats, sugar, almonds and a bottle of sherry and sent her hobbling on her way. In due course the ugly daughter met the hermit at the roadside, but when he asked for a share of her dinner she swore at him and made off as fast as she could. Justice was soon done, for the bad-tempered girl soon came to the brambly hedge and cut herself badly in trying to force her way through.

After the exertions forced on her by the hedge, the bad daughter sat down by the well for a rest. Of course the heads soon came up and repeated their rhyme to her, but she bashed each one soundly with her sherry bottle. The heads did not like this at all. This time their gifts were far from pleasant, even though the girl already had enough handicaps in life! The first head decided to give her leprosy on the face, the second wished bad breath upon her, and the third decided that marriage to a poor cobbler would just about serve her right.

Leaving the well behind, the girl limped on to the nearest town, which she reached in the middle of market day. The streets were crowded, but as people caught sight of her terrible face and smelled the first whiffs of her poisonous breath they fled screaming out of the town. Only one person was left, and that was a poor cobbler. The cobbler had just done a hermit a favour by mending his shoes, but the hermit had had nothing to pay him with. Instead of money, the cobbler had therefore accepted a bottle of leprosy ointment and a bottle of spirits that cured bad breath! One wonders if this was the same hermit who had shared lunch with the princess, now feeling sorry for her ugly step-sister! However, the cobbler offered the girl his medicines in exchange for her marrying him, and this she agreed to do.

One assumes that the ointment and the spirits worked, for the strange couple soon got married and journeyed to Colchester so that the cobbler could be introduced to his in-laws. The miserable old Queen was so furious to discover that her daughter had disgraced the family name by marrying a peasant that she hanged herself in shame and fury!

The King of Colchester was not worried at all by this. He had only married her for her money anyway, but he gave £100 to the ugly daughter and her poor husband on the condition that they went and lived in the remotest place they could find. This they did, and spent the rest of their lives working hard.

Was this a story about King Coel and Helena, who was said to be his daughter? One thing that links it with Helena is the appearance of the three heads and the gifts they bestowed. Saint Helena is said to have recovered the bodies of the three kings who brought the gifts to the baby Jesus. Two of these gifts – wealth (gold) and perfume (frankincense) are very similar to the gifts of the heads in the well. Whatever the meaning of the story, it is certain to have frightened many a child into being polite to strangers and not being malicious!

The
Prophet
of Gosfield

GOSFIELD is a small village a few miles north of Braintree, best known for its lake and the stately home which was visited by a succession of famous people. But it is also unique in having had its own prophet by the name of William Juniper. Most country prophets were distinctly dubious characters, but Juniper was respectable enough to be the subject of a short book written by the Bishop of Exeter in 1662.

What was the Bishop of a faraway place like Exeter doing writing about a remote village in Essex? The answer is simple, for the Bishop had once been 'Dean' (which is really just the local vicar) of Bocking, which is only a mile or two from Gosfield. Dr John Gauden was Dean from 1642 to 1660, but it was only after he left for Exeter that he wrote his short book called *The Strange & Wonderful Visions & Predictions of William Juniper*.

Although Juniper lived at Gosfield, he was a bricklayer by trade and often visited Bocking to work. A local man who Juniper did some work for told Dr Gauden about the bricklayer's strange dreams, emphasising that he seemed an honest man (there were a lot of fake prophets around in those days). Gauden hardly bothered to listen, deciding immediately that this Juniper must be 'crazy-minded'.

One morning in about 1649 Gauden was dozing peacefully

in bed when there was a loud knocking at the front door. A servant opened it and found Juniper there, pleading to speak with the Dean. Juniper was shown into the Dean's bedroom, where he told him that he had had a vision during the night. The effect of this was that Gauden must preach a sermon on 'Holiness to the Lord'. Juniper repeated this phrase three times and then left, saying that he had several other local clergy to see – even though it was pouring with rain. Gauden concluded from this visit that Juniper was 'more to be pitied than regarded.'

One of Gauden's neighbours, named Wentworth, told the clergyman that he should not dismiss Juniper so lightly. It was said that the Gosfield prophet had predicted the Revolution in the country, which had taken place when Parliament over-threw Charles I in the mid-1640s, and that he also predicted the Restoration of the Monarchy. Gauden kept hearing stories like this and after a while decided that it was time he found out for himself whether Juniper was mad or remarkable.

So he sent for him. Juniper, who seemed over sixty years old, struck Gauden as being honest and straightforward. Unlike many pseudo-prophets, he didn't seem to be making a big mystery out of it all. Gauden warned him that it was a very serious thing to claim to be God's prophet, and Juniper agreed. Then he began to describe his experiences.

Most of his visions began when he was asleep, Juniper said, but continued when he awoke. They were always very vivid and he never forgot the least detail of any of them. The first had occurred about seven years after he had got married. He prayed constantly for a child, then one day dreamed that he had a son, clearly seeing him wearing multi-coloured clothes as in a patchwork. Juniper told no-one of this dream, but shortly afterwards his wife became pregnant and in due course gave birth to a son. She made a garment for the little boy out of pieces of coloured cloth and thus it seemed to Juniper that his vision was proved correct. He was convinced that he had received this vision to show that his prayers were being answered.

33

The 1640s were years of trouble and warfare in England as the forces of King and Parliament struggled for supremacy. Armies marauded across the countryside and Colchester was besieged for weeks. Another of Juniper's visions seemed to him to reflect the troubles of the nation. In this dream he was out walking with two little beagles and was passing a house near a watermill when two great dogs called Full and Fat came out and attacked his beagles. Juniper defended his dogs with his staff but this was useless since Full and Fat were so well covered with flesh that they couldn't feel the strokes of his staff. Juniper called to the miller to control his dogs. The miller wasn't really interested, but did refer to Juniper's dogs as Will and Power. This, Juniper thought, was strange, because in his dream he was convinced that his own beagles were called Love and Obedience.

At this point Gauden interrupted the narrative, for he thought that all the names were rather strange for dogs. Juniper agreed, but explained that this was what they were in the dream. Juniper's explanation of the dream was that it reflected troubles in the nation and the Church of England. Perhaps he thought that love and obedience now counted for too little in the country.

King Charles I was beheaded in 1649, and Juniper said he had had a dream which seemed to predict this. He said he had dreamed that he was walking through the fields beside a hedge. When he looked over the hedge he saw a great crowd of soldiers and decided to climb up to higher ground to get a better view. Once at this viewpoint he realised that there was a battle going on. In the middle of it there was a man in rich robes, but smeared with blood. Even as Juniper watched, this man died from his wounds. Just then a woman in a rich mantle of purple rode up and threw herself on the dead body, tearing her hair out and weeping bitterly. Juniper felt that this represented the death of the King and the Church of England lamenting it.

In 1651 Charles I's son, Charles II, was defeated at Worcester and fled from England. Juniper said that in 1650 he had dreamed about this in a vision of a young lion in a field. The lion had been driven out of the field by asses, wolves, apes, foxes and horses, which afterwards all brayed in triumph.

In his next vision he dreamed he went into a church for the service but was disturbed to find chatting and playing of games going on in the congregation. He stood up to see if there were any other more religious men present and noticed some gentlemen; Juniper asked them if they would help to restore order, but they ignored him. When the minister arrived and climbed into a tiny pulpit the noise in the church carried on as if nothing had happened. So bad was it that Juniper could not hear a word that the minister said, and then a dark mist came down and hid the cleric from the congregation. Later, Juniper went out into the churchyard and found that all the grass had withered.

In his book, Gauden gives no commentary on this vision, but it is not hard to see what point lay behind it. The Church of England had suffered something of a battering when Oliver Cromwell controlled the country between 1653 and 1658, for Cromwell disagreed with a lot of its practices. Even respectable people, it seemed, were ignoring the Church – as a result of which the people would be cut off from the word of God and would wither like the grass!

In 1660 Charles II returned to England to take the throne. The meeting between Gauden and Juniper apparently took place several years before this occurred, but Juniper had already had a vision that predicted it. He said that he dreamed of a large field with a lion approaching it from the east. A mixture of beasts in the west prepared themselves for the lion's arrival with reverent and fawning attitudes. When the lion took up a place in the middle of the field the other animals prostrated themselves before it. Although the lion had been badly wronged by the other animals, it exacted no revenge on them.

Gauden said that Juniper died about a year after their meeting. He concluded his booklet by saying this about the Gosfield prophet:

'I did believe and do that there might be something of a Divine stroke or Beame sometimes, upon the good man's devout soul, whose heart and waies were so upright before God and so inoffensive before men.'

The Bishop's book was published in the first rush of enthusiasm after Charles II's return to England, and Juniper's predictions seemed to set a seal of Almighty approval on the King and the Church of England. Was it all a political ploy on the Bishop's part? It was certainly fortuitous for Gauden to choose that particular moment to bring the Prophet of Gosfield to the world's notice.

Doctor Swallow's Country Remedies

IF you had some spare cash and needed medical treatment in the 1640s, then you could ask William Swallow for assistance. Swallow was a doctor based at Great Dunmow and he treated patients across a wide area extending from Hatfield Broad Oak to Great Bardfield, and from Thaxted to Great Waltham.

Whether Swallow would have done you any good is another matter, of course. His training seems to have consisted largely of taking note of other people's ideas. Like many doctors in his day, Swallow was convinced that 'bleeding' a patient was a remedy for many ills; they believed that fevers were caused by too much blood or by bad blood, to which the natural solution was to get rid of the blood by having it sucked out by leeches. The fact that some patients survived such treatment was usually taken as evidence that it worked, which we can see from an extract from Swallow's notebooks:

'[A] famous doctor's apothecary told me that he bled the Earl of Lester's daughter after the small pox were come out, when she had above forty comed out upon her face and elsewhere, and he did it, and she did well.'

Smallpox was a deadly disease in those days. If a patient survived, they were likely to be scarred by 'pock-marks' on the skin – similar, but far worse, to the chickenpox that we are still familiar with today.

On one occasion Swallow was sent for to treat Lord Warwick's bailiff who was having fits. The Dunmow doctor treated him by applying plasters to the inside of his arms and pigeons, which cost one shilling each, to his feet. Swallow apparently picked the pigeon idea up from a London doctor.

Toothache was a common problem in the days when no-one ever brushed their teeth. In fact, if you still had a good set of teeth by the time you were thirty you were doing very well. Swallow had his own treatment for toothache, which involved making up a compound of four peppercorns, rosemary, and oyster shells powdered up. These ingredients were to be mixed with honey and vinegar and applied to the tooth 'in a fine ragge'.

A favourite prescription of Swallow's was 'snail-milk', but he also prescribed a number of fairly common substances like rhubarb. He was once told that convulsions could be cured by taking the heart, liver and lungs of a hare, drying them, and then beating them to a powder. Swallow tried this method but found it didn't work.

At times there doesn't seem to have been much difference between the ideas of the old country wives and Swallow's methods. He believed that boiling 'the blacke tops of crabbs clawes' was a powerful remedy, and also 'the bone that is found in the hearte of a ffarte' (apparently this was a hawk).

No doubt these remedies sometimes worked and sometimes didn't. It all depended on the state of mind of the patient. Some of the illnesses they contracted were quite strange as well – a Little Waltham woman claimed to have been poisoned by a spider, but was 'cured' by 'plaister of mithridate'.

Essex Serpents

IN these days of intensive farming and ever-spreading hous-
ing estates, you will be hard pressed to find any exotic
wildlife in Essex outside of Colchester zoo. Many centuries
ago, however, Essex seems to have gained something of a
reputation for being troubled by serpents, dragons and other
bizarre creatures, and there are several stories told about
them.

Two of the stories start with creatures being 'imported'
from abroad. One ancient legend deals with a great serpent
brought to England by Barbary merchants – probably from
the eastern Mediterranean. After arriving in London it somehow managed to escape and headed down the river Thames.
Now if it had continued going down the Thames it might have
been lost to Essex history for ever, but instead it came ashore
and took up residence on land. It lived between East Horndon
and Herongate, just to the south of Brentwood, and apparently spent many happy hours eating people.

Now this was obviously not a very satisfactory state of
affairs, and so Sir James Tyrell decided to sort the serpent out
for once and for all. Perhaps his wife didn't like the idea of him
doing such dangerous things, as he appears to have crept out
of the house one early morning without waking her. Now
everyone knows that serpents and dragons are very vain
creatures, so once Sir James had put on all his armour he hung
a mirror on his chest. Then he went off to slay the serpent.

It must have been just about breakfast time when the serpent saw the medieval equivalent of tinned food heading its way, so it soon rose up and got ready for battle. However, as soon as it looked at the knight it caught sight of its own reflection and was promptly mesmerised. This gave Sir James plenty of time to kill the serpent, and cut off its head. He took the head home with him and gave it to his wife when she woke up in the morning. It is not recorded whether she was very pleased!

Wormingford, in northern Essex, has a similar story, although in this case the creature was reputed to have been brought home by King Richard I after one of his crusades. It was called a cockadrille and was at first quite small. However, it grew up and escaped from London. Somehow it ended up in north Essex at Wormingford, perhaps having come up the Stour. Naturally, everyone was afraid of being chewed up by the fearful creature, so the Lord of the Manor – Sir George de la Haye – attacked and killed the creature in a field of the parish.

The nastiest of all the creatures seems to have been the Saffron Walden cockatrice. Exactly when it lived no one is certain, but it was a very long time ago. This creature turned up in the Meads near the town and proved to be a very venomous beast indeed. One source says that it was only a foot long but that it was yellowy-black in colour, had red eyes, a sharp head and a white spot on its crown. Apparently it didn't wind across the ground like other snakes but moved in a sort of upright position.

Despite its small size, this creature had a drastic effect on the neighbourhood. It was said that no herb could grow where it lived and that its breath was so foul and poisonous that it could break stones, blast plants and burn everything in its path. If a man touched it with a long pole it could still kill him and it could even kill a man from a distance just by looking at him. In fact it apparently killed so many people that Saffron Walden was almost depopulated!

Of course no creature like this could go unchallenged by a knight in shining armour, even if it was only a few inches high. However, such a strange and dangerous creature clearly called for imaginative tactics and the knight who eventually destroyed it wore a 'coat of christal glass'. Apparently the purity of the crystal was so repugnant to the foul little cockatrice that it curled up and died. The knight became a hero and his sword was hung up in the church where a brass effigy of the cockatrice was also placed. According to the legend, these interesting relics were destroyed by soldiers in the Civil War who thought they were part of some superstition. Maybe they were right!

The most recent serpent report in Essex was documented in a pamphlet published in 1669. On this occasion a 'venomous' creature was first seen in May 1668 at Birch Wood, Henham, not far from Lodge Farm. A man was riding by when the serpent rose up and terrified both rider and horse. Several miles later he got the horse under control and warned his friends – his immediate fear being that the creature would destroy the local cattle.

It was next seen by two passing men, though it was behaving in anything but a threatening manner. The creature seemed to be basking in the sun on top of a bank, allowing them a good view of it. It was estimated to be about eight or nine feet long and in its middle to be about as wide as a man's thigh. It had eyes the size of a sheep's, piercing white teeth, and wings only about two hands in length. Everyone agreed that these wings were much too small for it to fly, and indeed there are no reports of the strange creature having left the ground.

The two men were only carrying staves and didn't dare attack the creature; the serpent merely gazed at them peacefully. One went off to the lodge to get a gun whilst the other kept his eye on the creature from a safe distance. But then the serpent suddenly moved and dashed into the nearby wood, where it crashed around making a noise like a wild boar.

A group of people then got together to try to kill the creature, but whenever anyone approached it always retreated into the wood, and no one was brave enough to go in there in search of it. Though many were terrified of the creature, there was not a single report of it doing any harm, nor was it ever seen to eat anything. Whatever happened to it in the end, no one knows.

Essex certainly gained a name for itself as a place where serpents lived, even though the word 'serpent' seems to have been rather loosely given to any unfamiliar creature. For a time there were even two pubs in London called the 'Essex Serpent'. Perhaps it's time we had another serpent-sighting in Essex?

The Wanstead Heiress

CATHERINE Tylney Long seemed to have everything she could possibly desire – a huge annual income, youth and good looks, estates in Wiltshire, Hampshire and Essex . . . the list is endless. But when Catherine chose a husband to bring home to her palatial mansion in the then-delightful area of Wanstead, she chose badly; one fateful day in 1812 was to bring disaster on the family and would also hasten her own death.

Catherine was born in a humble inn at Chippenham in Wiltshire, but she was born into a far from humble position in life. In fact her lowly birth was due to her mother being caught unprepared whilst journeying to the family's country mansion at Draycot in Wiltshire. Her family were fabulously wealthy, for they had inherited the huge fortune built up by Sir Josiah Child, who had been chairman of the East India Company. As well as the house at Draycot, the family owned a mansion at Wanstead which had apparently been inspired by the chateau at Versailles; perhaps appropriately, it was generally rented out to Frenchmen like Louis XVIII.

In 1794 Catherine's brother died, and she became heir to the fortune. This was sufficient to generate an income of at least £60,000 per year and, when she took over the estate,

Catherine was reckoned to be the richest woman in Britain and a millionairess. Not surprisingly, pretty well every unmarried young nobleman in the land beat a path to her door. Her physical charms were rather limited – quite literally, since she was described as 'particularly petite', but it was her financial charms which attracted the suitors.

One of the foremost suitors was the Duke of Clarence, who was said to have proposed to her ten times and been rebuffed on each occasion. There was great surprise when Catherine finally decided on a husband, for she selected William Pole Wellesley, nephew of the Duke of Wellington and a notorious gambler and profligate.

The couple married at St James's church in Piccadilly in 1812. There were eight hundred guests and the wedding was conducted by the Rector of Wanstead. It was the 'Society' wedding of the year, and the bride dressed up to match her reputation as the richest woman in the land. She wore a dress of Brussels lace and white satin that cost 700 guineas, a bonnet of lace and ostrich feathers valued at 150 guineas, a veil that cost 200 guineas, and jewellery worth at least 25,000 guineas. Putting these prices into today's values, we may as well say that Catherine's outfit would have cost at least £1,000,000! After the wedding the couple lived at Wanstead, this presumably being more convenient for the social life of young nobility than the Wiltshire mansion.

Her husband changed his name following the marriage, becoming William Pole Tylney Long Wellesley. He was well-connected in his own right, and eventually succeeded to the titles of Baron Maryborough and Earl of Mornington. Quite what Catherine saw in him remains a mystery, for their married life was one long descent into disaster that began almost immediately. To celebrate his new Essex connections, Wellesley became Hereditary Warden of Waltham Forest and Patron of the Epping Hunt. When out on a hunt he delighted in scattering golden guineas to the poor who watched him ride by, but this was the least of his spendthrift habits.

Wellesley was a habitual gambler and seems to have had no

grasp of finances at all. Some people alleged that he spent his way through Catherine's fortune, but it seems more likely that he was only able to dispose of the annual income and not actually get rid of the estates. A lot of the money disappeared into various dens of vice in London, but he also spent a great deal on his political ambitions. These were the days before the Reform Act, and it was still quite normal for a man to buy his election. Wellesley spent huge sums in 1818 getting elected for Wiltshire.

Eventually Wellesley's behaviour caught up with him – and with poor Catherine. When they were away their house at Wanstead was seized to cover their debts, and its entire contents put under the hammer. A catalogue of its contents was prepared, and this ran to over four hundred pages; it took 32 days to sell everything, realising £41,000. Then the house itself was sold for building materials, fetching £9,550 and soon being demolished; it was a tragic loss for Wanstead.

Wellesley was not deflated by this blow. He had a notorious relationship with a Mrs Helena Bligh who he met whilst on a family trip to Italy. Catherine was so disgusted by her husband's open carousing with this woman that she returned home with their children. Wellesley was sued for adultery by Captain Bligh, the woman's husband, and was landed with £6,000 damages.

Catherine was a broken woman. Her reputation was destroyed, her income dissipated, her mansion lost. She died in 1825 at the age of only 35.

If it wasn't for Wellesley, Wanstead might still be in possession of one of the finest stately homes in the country, and Catherine Tylney might have lived longer and happier. But the mystery remains for ever: why on earth did she marry him?

The Curse
of the
Crooked Cross

MOST legends have a moral to them, and the moral of the story of the Crooked Cross is probably that it is a good idea to be polite and kind to people since you never know what they might do if you're not!

The story is said to be about a Friar from the Priory of Saint Botolph's in Colchester. In medieval times there were two religious houses very close to each other on the outskirts of Colchester, but now the remains of Saint Botolph's have almost been surrounded by shops.

The Friar in question was apparently called Brother Francis, and he was a well-intentioned but rather hot-tempered young man. Like many of the younger monks, he had not yet learnt the virtues of a peaceful disposition and a restrained tongue. One of his duties was to go into the market-place and buy food for the other Friars, and one particular Friday he was sent out to get fish, since monks were not allowed to eat meat on Fridays.

The best fish in the town could be bought from a stall run by an old crone called Dame Alice. Although her fish was good, Dame Alice drove a hard bargain and was often rude to her customers when they haggled over prices. In fact she was a classic 'fish-wife' (though many also said she was a witch).

This was the woman that Brother Francis had to deal with, and he soon got into a bad-tempered argument with her. After he had made his purchase, the Friar called back at her, 'Go to, you old baggage, you are no better than a witch.' The old woman didn't take too kindly to this comment. She told him that if she were indeed a witch then the curse of the crooked cross would alight on the shaven part of his head!

When he got back to the Priory, Brother Francis told his story to the other monks. Most of them thought it was a funny story, but one old monk was not so sure. He told Francis to pray for forgiveness and to ask the Prior's permission to touch the piece of the True Cross that was kept on the High Altar.

Francis was worried that the old monk had taken the fish-wife's curse seriously, but he didn't want any of the others to learn of his fears. For the rest of the day he worried about what the 'Crooked Cross' could possibly mean, but the hours went by without anything strange happening to him. Just as dusk arrived, though, some of the other monks noticed that strange marks were beginning to appear on Francis' shaven head – dark, rough hair had suddenly started to grow and was forming into two crooked lines that crossed in the middle of his head.

The Prior, who was meditating in his garden, was called. He ordered that the head should be shaven once more and then washed with holy water. But even this treatment made no difference, for as soon as the hair was shaved off it began to grow again; some monks even said that there was a faint smell of brimstone as they shaved it! Francis had to confess to the Prior that he had had hard words with Dame Alice, and he was told to spend all night meditating in front of the High Altar as a penance. Some other monks were told to watch over him during the night, and they reported next morning that they had seen strange blue lights flickering in the hair of the crooked cross which had grown a full inch overnight.

The other monks were afraid of him and so the Prior had Francis confined to his cell. The Magistrates were sent for and, after inspecting Francis and listening to his tale, they decided to arrest the old woman on a charge of witchcraft. The monks did their best to stop the story getting out, but soon St Botolph's was besieged by people curious to see the branded monk. Some even said that all the monks were affected, and that the monastery walls themselves were marked with the curious sign.

The old woman was locked up in Colchester Castle but was entirely unrepentant. She said it had served Francis right and that she would curse the Prior too if he wasn't careful. Many other people came forward to tell tales about the old woman and so she was found guilty and condemned to death.

While she lay in the dungeons many efforts were made to remove the mark from Francis, but all were unsuccessful. The night before she was due to be executed a confessor came to speak to Alice, but during his visit she worked herself up into such a rage that she had a fit and died. From this moment on the crooked cross ceased to grow, and when Francis's head was shaved again it never re-appeared. The old woman was buried outside the town walls by night and Francis, it was said, never used harsh words against anyone for the rest of his life!

The Nine Day Wonder

THESE days we are all familiar with the strange sort of things that people do to raise money for charity. However, there can have been few exploits as unusual as William Kemp's journey from London to Norwich in the late 1500s.

William Kemp was a famous actor. As well as appearing in several of Shakespeare's plays, it is quite likely that he was personally acquainted with the bard. Kemp was best known for his comedy roles and also for his dancing, as a result of which he conceived a bizarre plan to dance all the way from London to Norwich with bells on his feet.

It seems unlikely that Kemp decided to do this for charity, so we can't credit him with inventing the sponsored dance. Perhaps he decided on his strange journey out of a mixture of a sense of fun and to create a bit of publicity for himself. He also wrote a booklet about the journey, so no doubt he also made a few shillings from that.

He laid the plans for his journey in 1599. There were two people appointed to accompany him – Thomas Slye, his taborer, who also had a pipe, and an overseer to check that Kemp kept to his word.

He decided to start from the City of London, and may have been seen off officially by the Lord Mayor. Kemp started early in the day, at about 7 am, but even so there were plenty of people around to see him away and he had difficulty in dancing his way through the crowds. What a strange sight the small procession must have been – the actor leaping about as his bells jingled, the taborer intent on striking up a jaunty tune, and the officious overseer strolling along behind. Large numbers of young men tried to follow on too, but Kemp's pace was altogether too athletic for most of them.

At Bow he was wise enough to refuse an offer of an alcoholic beverage, but there were further distractions laid on at Stratford – then the first real town into Essex of course. It was known that Kemp was a devotee of bear-baiting, the rather unpleasant sport in which terriers and bulldogs were set on tethered bears, so a bear had been arranged to entertain him at Stratford. However Kemp was full of the first flush of enthusiasm for his journey, and hardly gave the bear a glance.

Instead he carried on to Ilford, where he had a brief rest, and then proceeded to Romford where he spent two nights. Clearly he was not racing to Norwich, since he had several lengthy stays at various towns along the route. No doubt he earned more money by giving shows at each place.

Leaving Romford he strained his hip, and poor Kemp was in agony by the time he stopped for a rest at Brentwood. Nonetheless he pressed on and reached Ingatestone for the night. By this time he had accumulated a fair number of hangers-on, not all of whom were particularly desirable characters. Amongst the large crowds were several 'cutpurses' and pickpockets, two of whom were arrested at Brentwood.

He spent his next night at Chelmsford, which must suggest that he was already getting weary since each 'leg' of the journey was getting progressively shorter! Further evidence for his weariness is that when the Chelmsford people demanded a performance of the famous dancing, Kemp locked himself in his inn room rather than fulfil their wishes.

After Chelmsford he diverged from the main road to head towards Braintree. Perhaps this was a bad decision since the road proved to be very low quality! There were deep holes full of water, in some of which he landed up to his waist. Two young men who tried to keep up with him also got stuck in the mud. It is of one of these roads around Braintree that the tale is told of a gentleman who was riding on horseback, splashing carelessly through the puddles. Imagine the gentleman's surprise when he spurred the horse onwards into what he thought was just another puddle – only for the horse to disappear completely into it! Sadly it is said that the horse was drowned and the rider was lucky to escape with his life.

Under these circumstances Kemp must have been glad to reach Braintree, where he stopped for two days of rest. He was full of praise for the hospitality of the inhabitants of the town, who can rarely have had such a strange visitor. Then he carried on through Clare to Bury St Edmunds, where he was delayed by snow. After Thetford he arrived at the gates of Norwich, but decided to delay his entry whilst the Mayor arranged a special ceremony and whilst he refreshed himself.

The next day the Mayor arranged for the turnpike to be specially opened and for a triumphal entry into the city. The journey had taken him four weeks, of which only nine days had been spent in dancing. But it had certainly caught the public imagination, and Kemp went on to give dancing demonstrations in Europe. One rumour even has it that he danced over the Alps!

Hero
or
Villain?

RIGHT in the north-eastern corner of Essex, in Dovercourt churchyard, is the tomb of a man whose death caused international controversy. His name was Charles Algernon Fryatt, and he was employed by the Great Eastern Railway as captain of one of its North Sea ferries. He was given a hero's farewell at St Paul's Cathedral and many famous and important people accompanied his body back to Essex for burial. Yet some would say that Fryatt was not a hero at all; instead they claim that he broke the Geneva Convention and should be counted a war criminal.

Charles Fryatt was born at Southampton in 1872 but he moved to Harwich when he was still a child since his father got a job on the Great Eastern Railway's steamer *Cambridge* as first officer. Young Fryatt went to the Corporation School in Harwich and then, naturally, turned to the sea for a career. In 1892 he signed up as a seaman on the GER's *Ipswich* and made the first of many trips across the North Sea from Harwich or Parkeston to the Continent.

Fryatt rose steadily through the ranks of the GER's merchant navy and eventually was given command of the *Colchester*. In 1913 he was transferred to become Master of the *Newmarket*, which worked the Harwich to Rotterdam cargo run.

When World War One broke out in the late summer of 1914 it had a sudden and dramatic effect on the regular routines of men like Fryatt. The GER's services continued to run to the Netherlands but Harwich itself became a naval base and the last passenger ferry left it on 6th August; among the passengers was Count von Bulow, the German ambassador, returning home.

The First World War marked the first use of submarines on a major scale, and the GER ships from the Essex ports were soon having their problems in maintaining the service to neutral Holland. In May 1915 the *Colchester* was chased by a U-boat when only two miles off Harwich and in August a torpedo passed right underneath the *Cromer* and out the other side; the U-boat then chased the GER ferry for twenty miles, but the superior speed of the ship eventually saved it.

Fryatt was in the thick of things right from the start. In March 1915 he was in charge of the *Wrexham*, which had been loaned to the GER by the Great Central Railway. A U-boat on the surface signalled him to stop, but Fryatt ignored the signal and steamed at 16 knots through shoals and mines to escape. He was awarded a gold watch in commemoration of this achievement.

Barely three weeks later he was commanding the *Brussels* when a U-boat was sighted near the Maas Light Vessel. This time Fryatt proved unable to escape by using speed and seemed to be in real danger of being torpedoed as the U-boat submerged. Instead, he turned his ship towards the last position of the submarine and attempted to ram it as it dived.

There was much debate over whether Fryatt was successful or not, but it seems most likely that the U33 had escaped as there were no marks on the hull of the *Brussels*. Fryatt was rewarded with another watch and the story received great attention in the press.

Later events called into question the wisdom of Fryatt's actions. As a non-combatant he was contravening the Geneva Convention in taking violent action against the enemy. Another possible consequence of this may have been that

U-boat commanders were less likely to give civilian vessels the opportunity to surrender before attacking them.

In June 1916 Fryatt was still in command of the *Brussels* when it left Hook of Holland with refugees and cargo on board. However, it never reached Essex and two days later reports began to come in that it had been captured by the Germans and taken to Zeebrugge, a Belgian port that was in their control. Though the subsequent events caused a sensation in Britain, it took several years for the full story to emerge.

It seems likely that the Germans deliberately tracked the *Brussels* as it left the Hook. Fryatt and his vessel were intercepted by five destroyers and torpedo boats at 1.30 am on June 3rd 1916. Armed German seamen climbed aboard and smashed the radio. Then most of the English crew were taken off and the Germans installed their own commander. When they rang down to the engine room for the *Brussels* to start there was no response – the engine room crew had been taken off as well! When the Germans got the ship going again, they headed it back towards Zeebrugge. *Brussels* stayed five hours at Zeebrugge and was then taken to Bruges. The crew of forty men and five women were locked up together for two nights in a cell under Bruges Town Hall. Everyone was then taken by cattle train to Ghent, where another night was spent in a slimy cellar. The stewardesses, mostly Essex women, were taken from Ghent to Cologne, kept for a short while in a camp at Holzminden, then repatriated via the Dutch border.

The men were less fortunate – they were scattered around several different prisoner-of-war camps and had to wait until the end of hostilities before they saw Britain again. However Fryatt and First Officer Hartnell were separated from the others at Ruhleben, and taken back to Bruges for questioning. Someone high up in the German command had clearly discovered that Fryatt was no ordinary merchant seaman.

A naval court was set up, presided over by Commander von Yorke. Fryatt was charged with having attacked the U33 while he was a non-combatant; his inscribed watches and English press cuttings were used as evidence against him, supporting the argument that he had deliberately attacked the submarine and had been rewarded for having done so. The tone of some of the British papers can hardly have helped him in this matter.

The captain of the U33 did not turn up to give evidence although it was said that he was going to, so Fryatt never discovered how close his attack had come to success.

Fryatt was found guilty and sentenced to death by firing squad to be carried out that same evening. Fryatt was taken out and placed before sixteen riflemen. He must have died instantly, and then his body was buried in Bruges cemetery under a plain black cross. The Germans posted a notice to explain the execution:

'NOTICE – The English Captain of the Mercantile Marine, Charles Fryatt, of Southampton, though he did not belong to the armed forces of the enemy, attempted on

56

March 28th 1915, to destroy a German submarine, running it down. This is the reason why he has been condemned to death by judgment of this day of the War Council of the Marine Corps and has been executed. A perverse action has thus received its punishment, tardy but just.

Signed VON SCHRODER, Admiral Commandant of the Corps de Marine, Bruges, July 27th 1916.'

When rumours of the execution began to filter through to England, there was a storm of outrage. The Imperial Merchant Service Guild called it 'the most despicable crime yet perpetrated by Germany'.

The rumours were confirmed by Prime Minister Asquith in July, when he stated in Parliament, 'I deeply regret to say that it appears to be true that Captain Fryatt has been murdered by the Germans.' The truth of the reports had been checked through the American embassy, since the USA was still neutral at that stage of the war.

Lord Claud Hamilton of the Great Eastern Railway observed that 'the latest act of the Hun is nothing less than sheer, brutal murder'. His Company awarded Mrs Fryatt, who had seven children, a pension of £25 per year, to which the Government added £100.

The Mayor of Harwich opened a memorial fund and a Captain Fryatt memorial was put up in the booking hall at Liverpool Street station in 1917, where it can still be seen today though it could do with smartening up a little.

The *Brussels* itself remained at Zeebrugge until it was sunk by the British *Dover Patrol* raid of October 1917. After the war it was salvaged and put to use in the Irish Sea.

Fryatt's body was exhumed at the end of hostilities and brought back to England. He was given a hero's farewell at St. Paul's and then buried in Essex within sight of the Stour estuary, out of which he had commanded so many ships.

Osyth
the
Essex Saint

A FEW miles east of Colchester, looking down onto the estuary of the river Colne, is the small village of Saint Osyth's. The history of Dark Age England is full of stories of saints that most people have forgotten, none more interesting than the story of Essex's own Saint Osyth who lived in the mid-600s AD.

If Osyth had been born today it would probably have been said that she was 'well-connected', for her father was Frithewald, the first Christian king of the East Angles. Frithewald clearly took his religion seriously, because he obviously made sure that his daughter was brought up a true Christian herself. When she was still quite young he arranged for her to be sent north to the Burton-on-Trent district to be educated, and this is when the first extraordinary event in her life is said to have happened.

Perhaps she was such an innocent child that she had not learnt about danger, but somehow poor little Osyth fell into a river whilst in the north and was drowned. For three days her body stayed in the water before it was recovered, pale white and very definitely dead. However, Modwen, a Saxon woman who was later declared a saint herself, prayed for the little girl to recover and miraculously she did.

This should have shown everyone that Osyth was marked out for a life rather different from the ordinary, but her parents clearly did not appreciate this. Although Osyth really wanted to devote her life to God and enter a convent, her father arranged for her to marry Sighere, the King of Essex.

A wedding feast was duly arranged, to which Sighere turned up with all his friends and relatives. However, halfway through the meal Sighere caught sight of a proud stag over by the woods; this was too much of a temptation for him, since he and his friends were passionately keen on hunting. Forgetting his duties and his bride, Sighere dashed outside to begin the chase.

To Osyth this must have seemed like a heaven-sent opportunity. She too left the wedding feast, and went straight away to a nearby religious house. Sighere returned to find her gone but, according to the legend, he was a wise man and realised that if she had given her heart to God he would not be able to compete.

Osyth endowed the convent she had fled to with land, and in due course rose to become its Abbess. There she lived a peaceful life for quite a few years until in the year 653 a band of savage Danes sailed into the creek of the river Colne which her convent overlooked. Not having any respect for Christianity, the Danes ransacked the convent for anything of value, and doubtless annoyed the nuns somewhat as well.

They did not find the Abbess however, so their leaders Inguar and Hubba began a search for her. They eventually found Osyth standing by a fountain in a nearby wood, and demanded that she accompany them to their ship. She refused, and one of the Vikings drew his sword; with one stroke he beheaded her.

Inguar and Hubba must have been astonished when, as calmly as if nothing of any significance had happened, Osyth bent down and picked up her head! Carrying it carefully, she walked over to a nearby church and knocked firmly on the door, her white hands stained with her own blood. Only then did she collapse dead on the threshold of the church.

Where her head fell, a fountain of water immediately started to gush out of the earth, as if the ground itself was weeping over her death. Later a monument was put up at this point and it was said that the water continued to flow for several hundred years.

Osyth's body was not immediately buried in the church, as it had seemed to want, but was instead taken to Aylesbury which was near where she was born. Only forty years later was it returned and interred in a precious casket at the place she had loved. The ceremony was conducted by the Bishop of London with help from the Bishop of Rochester; the latter had suffered from an illness for many years and this was miraculously healed during the service.

This is the legend of Saint Osyth, and for many years there was a religious house there. Not all the abbots were so pious as Osyth had been – in the time of Richard II one was imprisoned at Colchester for poaching on the king's land and stealing his venison. The abbey was, of course, eventually closed down by the orders of Henry VIII, but Osyth's name still lives on at that place.

The City of Wisdom

'THE City of Wisdom' seems a rather exotic name for a place in Essex, but it is in fact a name once given to the small market town of Coggeshall. The name was given to it – rather sarcastically – in a ballad which lampooned the Coggeshall residents for being rather dim-witted. This reputation has given rise to a whole set of stories about the stupid things that Coggeshall people have done, grouped together under the title of 'Coggeshall Jobs'.

It is certainly a reputation that has been around for some time, since a rhyme as long ago as the 1600s said this about some local towns:

> 'Braintree for the pure
> And Bocking for the poor,
> Coggeshall for the jeering town
> And Kelvedon for the whore.'

The last line of this tended to get amended to 'bore' instead of 'whore' to suit more sensitive dispositions.

At one time there were a series of ballads and plays made up about the activities of the Coggeshall people and in particular their force of volunteer soldiers. These amateur troops were

gathered together in the early 1800s to defend the town in case Napoleon Bonaparte invaded, but they suffered from the classic problem of too many officers and not enough 'other ranks'. In fact there was only one Private in the entire force, and he was so dim as to cause real problems in organising a parade. The poor man could never remember which leg was his left and which was his right, so his officers tied a piece of hay to one leg and a piece of straw to the other and marched him along by calling out 'Hay, straw, hay, straw'!

The Volunteers were the subject of a play written by Thomas Harris who himself may have made something of a 'Coggeshall Job' of it. Harris was employed as the local schoolmaster and obviously a play pointing out the stupidity of the local people would not exactly endear him to his employers. The result was that Harris was sacked.

Another story about Coggeshall is not strictly speaking to do with Jobs at all, but is interesting all the same. Many years ago, it is said, Bishop Porteous was travelling through Coggeshall when he saw a massive crowd all gathered together. He immediately made enquiries as to what was going on, and was informed that it was the annual Coggeshall Lying Contest. Being a rather pious man, the Bishop was horrified that anything like this should exist. He was told that the Jury awarded a prize of a whetstone to whoever most impressed them with the quality of their lying.

The Bishop decided to put a stop to this heathen and sinful practice immediately. He got out of his carriage and marched over to the centre of the gathering. He launched into a passionate sermon about the wickedness of lying and told the crowd how pleased he was that he had never told a lie in his life. Imagine the Bishop's consternation when the Jury immediately awarded him the prize for being the most daring liar! They directed that the whetstone should be placed in his carriage; apparently the Bishop later saw the funny side of this and had the stone placed on his mantelpiece.

But back to Coggeshall Jobs. A lot of them have been repeated many times, so this is just a selection. There was one about a man who wanted to move a tree to a different position, so in order to make digging its roots up easier he cut it down first!

On another occasion the Coggeshall people decided to go and get some fish from the lake at Gosfield, about six miles away. They took some buckets full of water with them to bring the fish back in – not realising that they could have filled the buckets up when they got to Gosfield.

One year a dog went mad in Coggeshall and went around snarling and growling in a frightful manner. In the end it bit a wheelbarrow, so for safety the Coggeshall people locked up the wheelbarrow in a shed in case that too went mad.

When a calf got its head stuck between the bars of a field gate, the Coggeshall farmer's remedy was to send for a saw. He didn't use this to cut the gate bars though, but sawed off the head of the calf so that the animal could walk free.

Coggeshall used to have two windmills, but it was often observed that the sails were hardly turning round as the breeze was so slight. The Coggeshall people concluded that this was because there was not enough wind for two mills and so they knocked one down.

These tales are quite unfair of course, and the present day citizens of Coggeshall rightly insist that whatever their reputation in the past its current population are as sensible as everyone else!

The Silent Man

WILLIAM Kempe was born in the district around Finch-ingfield in about 1555. In 1588 he married Philippa Gunter and moved to Spains Hall, quite an impressive house that can still be found today. They had only one child, a girl called Jane.

Their married life seems to have been dominated by one problem – William's foul temper. No matter how hard he tried, every so often he would lose his temper and let out a torrent of abuse, which he usually directed at his wife. One day in 1621 he had provoked a fierce row on account of his own jealousy – he seems to have accused her of seeing another man, though they were both well into old age by this time it would seem. Nonetheless William let out a stream of cruel words which hurt his wife deeply; then, suddenly racked by remorse, he ran off to seek the quiet of the woods.

Pacing around between the trees, William agonised over his faults. All of a sudden he realized what he must do – if his tongue caused the problem, then his tongue must suffer. There and then he vowed not to speak at all for seven years.

The last words he spoke were his vows to remain silent. These words were overheard by one of the dubious characters who used to inhabit the remote woodlands of Essex at that time, one who was known as 'the Raven'. Raven was wander-ing around the woods making up potions when he overheard

Kempe making his vow, and he confronted the wretched man. Raven warned him that he had better abandon his vow there and then, for no good would come of it. Kempe steadfastly shook his head, so Raven went on to warn Kempe that if he lived to see the end of the seven years he might find it impossible to speak at all.

Kempe dismissed Raven's words as the mumbo-jumbo of one who spent too much time muttering about witches and potions. Instead he went home to Spains Hall, where his family were intensely confused by his silence. Fearing that a spell had been cast on him they sent for the vicar who prayed for him, then they sent for the physician who could think of no treatment for such a strange disease. After a while William was able to convince them all of the reason for his silence. He took to writing out messages, and trained a man-servant to recognise his own sort of sign language. Nothing was going to shake him from the vow he had taken.

Despite his advancing age, Kempe decided to mark each year of his vow by digging a fish pond at the back of the Hall. By the end of his seven years he would have seven ponds, each stocked with a different type of fish. However, the year after he had taken the vow three of his servants were drowned; they may well have died in his fishpond, but there was also a moat around the Hall which could have claimed them.

Perhaps this made Kempe think of the Raven's words, but certainly they must have been brought to mind when his wife died in 1623. Even when she was dying he steadfastly refused to break his vow of silence, and it is hardly likely that his refusal to talk had made her any happier than she had been before.

The following year William Kempe was out riding his horse when the animal stumbled and threw him. His leg was badly injured and he was unable to move. He was also unable to call out for help, due to his vow of silence, and so lay on the cold, damp ground all through a rainy night. Only the next morning did another traveller come across him and help to get him back to Spains Hall.

In the winter of 1626 Kempe went to a nearby market town to settle some business, taking the servant who understood his sign language with him. Leaving the town to start the journey home, it was clear that a storm was gathering and it was already getting gloomy. Kempe was confident that they could make the seven or so miles to Spains Hall before the worst of the storm broke, but he was wrong. Soon the weather was so bad that the two men had to seek shelter in a ruined castle nearby.

They tethered their horses in a sheltered spot outside, then went up the steps into the old keep. They were surprised to find a fire still smouldering inside, but concluded that tramps or wanderers had passed this way.

The servant lay down and was soon fast asleep, but Kempe was restless and was also worried about the fire. As he sat there in the darkness, he fancied that he could hear the sound of muffled voices from the room above. Leaving the servant asleep, he crept up the old stone staircase that went up inside the thick walls of the keep. He tiptoed up one flight, then another, until he was at the floor above where he fancied the voices were coming from. Carefully he lay down and put his ear to the floor, straining to hear what was happening below.

He was right! There were people below and, what was more, they seemed to be robbers planning a raid. Kempe must have been astonished when he heard one of the robbers name the target for that night's attack – Spains Hall!

Quickly and silently he crept downstairs again. There was no time to explain to the servant what was happening, since he could only do this by writing, and so Kempe just hustled the poor man outside as fast as he could. They climbed onto their horses as fast as possible, then set off at full speed towards Spains Hall.

It had been raining heavily for hours, and soon they came to a ford that was made virtually impassable by a torrential river. An old man like Kempe had no hope of getting across, though the younger servant was willing to give it a try. Hurriedly Kempe wrote the details of what he had discovered on a piece of paper, which he gave to the servant; the young man then plunged into the river, not even having the time to read the note.

Whilst Kempe tried to find an alternative route home, the young servant rode straight to the Hall. When he arrived, however, it was found that the note had been saturated by the river water and was quite unreadable. The servants discussed the situation, and decided that the old man must be in some serious trouble, so they got themselves together and went out into the dark, stormy night in search of him.

The desperate band of robbers were not at all frightened by the weather. Indeed the darkness of the night and the howling of the wind were a perfect cover for their villainous plans. Nor were they halted by the torrent, but plunged their horses into the river with reckless abandon. When they reached Spains Hall they couldn't believe their luck, for the house seemed empty and so they started plundering it of all the valuables.

One of the robbers went upstairs to rifle the bedrooms. Creeping into one of the rooms, he was surprised by a sudden movement in a corner and immediately fired his pistol. The body of a little boy slumped at his feet.

The events of this terrible night must have reawakened Kempe's memories of the Raven's prophecy, but he still kept to his vow. Finally, in 1628, his work was finished and the last of the seven fishponds was complete. The seven years were almost over and Kempe, now seventy-three years old, went gladly upstairs for his last night under the vow of silence. His heart was full of joy, and no doubt he was thinking over what his first words would be.

His sleep was not restful though, and he was troubled by disturbing dreams. He awoke in the morning feeling feverish and was horrified to discover that he could not move his body at all. Kempe opened his mouth to cry for help, but no words would come. When the servants came up to see why he hadn't appeared he was unable to even write a message. During the day his condition deteriorated and later that day poor William

Kempe died. The Raven's words had come true, for disaster had certainly followed him ever since he had made his vow of silence.

The
Duchess
of Romance

WHEN it comes to thinking of novelists connected with Essex, most people can think of Dorothy L. Sayers, but few would ever recall the name of Margaret, Duchess of Newcastle. But not only did Margaret write numerous books, she also devised a style of plot that seems to have anticipated the pulp fiction of the 1980s by three hundred years. If she had been alive today, Margaret would have been writing novels of breathy romance or pumping out the lurid prose for torrid paperbacks.

Margaret was born into the Lucas family of Colchester in 1623. They lived at St John's Abbey since her grandfather had bought up the estate there after the Dissolution. Thus she was born into a situation where she never needed to worry about anything and, being the youngest daughter, was hopelessly spoilt. Much of her childhood she seems to have filled by writing books, sixteen of them before she was twelve years old!

In 1642, just as trouble between King Charles I and Parliament was coming to a head, Margaret conceived an ambition to become a lady of the court. Her mother was not at all keen on this, but was quite unable to say no to her spoilt daughter. Thus Margaret went off to become a maid of honour to Queen Henrietta Maria, though she was desperately unhappy to begin with. For a girl who had been cocooned at home and treated as something special, being just one among hundreds must have come as a shock!

Nonetheless, when the Queen went to Paris to escape the Civil War, Margaret Lucas went with her. The war was to prove tragic for her family, for in 1648 her brother, Sir Charles, was shot by Parliamentary forces at the end of the siege of Colchester.

For the time being, though, Margaret threw herself into the life of the court at Paris. It was now that love entered her life, for in 1645 she was introduced to the Marquis of Newcastle. The Marquis was a widower thirty years older than Margaret, but he had a sharp eye when it came to spotting an attractive wench. He focused on Margaret straight away, particularly entranced by her full and generous figure. When addressing her he often referred lasciviously to her 'plump flesh'.

It was not the Marquis' physique that attracted Margaret, but his fame and reputation, for he had been commander of the Royalist forces in the North until they had been defeated at the battle of Marston Moor. To a young and impressionable girl he thus combined all the virtues of fame, steadfastness and maturity, so it was not long before love blossomed.

After they married, the couple settled in Antwerp for a while, worrying over their debts and longing for the day when they would be able to return to England. Newcastle had ambitions to become a playwright so Margaret revived her own literary pretensions as well. Together they filled in the empty hours by writing literature of a dubious quality.

If Margaret were alive today, her fiction would net her a huge fortune, for she combined all the features now so popular in the sort of paperbacks that contain at least six hundred pages and locations that spread around the world. One of her books was called *Assaulted and Pursued Chastity*, which she claimed to have written 'to show young women the danger of travelling without their parents'. It was the sort of book that most upper class parents of the time would *not* have shown their children!

The book featured a well-bred orphan girl named Lady Affectionata; lack of one or both parents was a feature of most of Margaret's heroines. Lady Affectionata sets out on a voyage but is shipwrecked on a rocky coast, which proves to be part of the Kingdom of Sensuality. The Prince of Sensuality specialises in ruining young maidens, and Affectionata soon falls into his clutches. However, before anything serious can happen, she manages to escape dressed as a young man and using the name of Travelia. She takes another ship, encounters more problems with lustful males, then is wrecked again. This time she is in a land where the royals have orange skin, black hair and white nails. They turn out to be sun-worshippers and are just about to sacrifice Affectionata when she manages to shoot the High Priest and escape! Whilst all this is going on, the lustful Prince keeps trying to catch up with her; this he eventually manages to do – but only after they've got married.

As Newcastle was a 'dramatist', Margaret explored this avenue as well. One of her plays was entitled *Love's Adventures*, and combined the usual blend of passionate pot-boiling. This time it featured two young ladies, Lady Bashful and Lady Orphan. Lady Bashful meets Sir Serious Dumb and falls in love, whereupon she ceases to be bashful and he becomes talkative. Lady Orphan falls in love with Lord Singularity and, amidst a complicated series of adventures, is invited to Rome by the Pope. There she addresses the entire College of Cardinals, who have got some bad ideas, and wins them over by her brilliantly intellectual arguments.

There is much in Margaret's work which was typical of the 'Restoration comedies' which came to vogue after Charles II was restored to the throne in 1660. Certainly it was often pointed out that Margaret's plays contained rather a lot of adultery and seduction. Several of her published works were produced with a frontispiece depicting the lady herself – often in a low-cut dress revealing her well-formed bosom!

The Newcastles returned to England in 1660, following which the Marquis was made a Duke in recognition of his services to the king. Margaret threw herself into London life with great enthusiasm, seeing it as a great opportunity to pursue her literary interests. She attended a performance of one of her husband's plays and, at the close, ostentatiously thanked the actors from her box. The play was called *Humorous Lovers* and Margaret dressed for it in clothes that she had made herself. Being too vain to take advice, these were a long way out of fashion and were described by Pepys as 'antique dress'.

Her clothes attracted a great deal of attention because of their peculiarity. They were always her own designs and bore no relation to what the other court ladies were wearing. At one time she wore a velvet cap with long falling feathers that obscured her face; she explained that the fanning motion of the feathers cooled her face.

Nonetheless her company was much sought-after. Samuel Pepys made efforts for several days to even see her, having heard tell of her shapeliness. When he at last saw her he was a little disappointed that she was no longer in the prime of her beauty.

Opinion was sharply divided over her personality. Pepys concluded that she was 'a mad, ridiculous conceited woman'. This was an opinion shared by Evelyn and his wife; the former concluded that she was a 'mighty pretender to learning, poetrie and philosophie' but highly entertaining all the same. His wife considered that Margaret was the most extravagant and conceited person she had ever come across. She complained particularly about the Duchess of Newcastle's conversation which seems to have matched her books, describing it as 'airy, empty . . . terminating commonly in nonsense, oaths, and obscenity'.

In order to branch out from fiction, the Duchess tried her hand at 'philosophy' as well, and explored scientific ideas. This, though, did not really satisfy the hot-blooded side of her nature.

She died in 1673, and the Duke died three years later. But Margaret, Duchess of Newcastle should not be dismissed entirely as the talented and conceited woman that Pepys judged her to be. Charles Lamb, the writer and man of letters, championed her, calling her 'the thrice noble, chaste, and virtuous, – but again somewhat fantastical, and original-brain'd, generous, Margaret Newcastle'.

She was buried in Westminster Abbey and an effigy of her at rest created; not many Essex women can claim that honour, especially not ones with a reputation for obscene language and books full of adultery!

The Power
Behind
The Throne

IN the year 1400 there was a rather unusual funeral in the
little village of Upminster. Alice de Windsor, lady of the
manor at Gaynes, near Upminster, was laid to rest with all the
usual ceremony. But there were one or two things which set
her funeral out from the rest; money was distributed to the
poor on her funeral day as she had stipulated in her will, and
also money was left to repair the local roads. This was unusual
enough, but the really important thing about Alice was that
she had at one time been the most influential woman in the
land – and some said her influence had been far from bene-
ficial.

Where did she come from? There are several versions of the
story, the least kind suggesting that she was a woman of 'low
birth' who was the daughter of an Essex tiler. For a while she
had worked as a domestic servant of a low class, but had then
somehow risen to influence – perhaps through witchcraft.

Another tale says that she was the daughter of a Devon
weaver, but the most likely explanation is that she came from
the Perrers family of Hertfordshire, who were important
enough to have had an M.P. among their number.

Alice became a lady of the Queen's bedchamber, which
suggests that she was of noble birth in some way. This brought

her to the attention of the king, Edward III, and by 1366 she had become his mistress. Edward rewarded her with valuable goods, including wine and jewels. No doubt Alice was pleased to see the death of the Queen in 1369.

With the Queen out of the way, Alice was able to use her charms to create a tidy little fortune for herself. The King seemed to be hopelessly ensnared by her beauty, and she used this to gain property for herself by unlawful means. The Essex manors of Gaynes and Steeple St Lawrence soon became hers. Protected by the king's influence, she was quite prepared to interrupt the judges in the courts and give them her own opinion!

One thing that Alice loved above all was to dress up and be admired. With the King's money to play with, she could pursue this interest as much as she liked. A jousting competition was the perfect occasion to put on a display, so one day in 1375 she dressed up as a Lady of the Sun and rode through London from the Tower to Smithfield, attracting admiration everywhere.

Alice's influence over the King was a cause of much jealousy and suspicion. She had quite turned Edward's head, as a result of which the government of the country was becoming a disgrace. Some were convinced that this was witchcraft, and that Alice must be stopped.

In 1376 the 'Good Parliament' met and, supported by Edward's son, the Black Prince, told the King that Alice was a married woman. The result of this was that she was temporarily banished, but Alice got her own back by helping to disgrace the Speaker of the House of Commons.

So by 1377 she was back in favour, though her plots and machinations continued as before. She was alleged to have got a squire to murder a sailor, then used her influence to protect him from prosecution.

Alice was clever enough to know that her influence would only last as long as Edward lived. By 1377 he was very ill, and she visited him whilst he was on his death bed. She did her best to make him believe that he would recover, talking of hunts that he would go on and feasts that he would enjoy. But, so it is said, she herself knew that he was dying and, as he slipped in and out of fevered sleep, stole the gold rings off his fingers.

When the King died she 'retired' to Upminster. This was a wise move, for any further involvement in London politics without the King's support could have been disastrous. She had already had a narrow escape in 1376 when a friar, said to be her accomplice in witchcraft, had been arrested.

The last twenty years of Alice's life seem to have passed quietly, and as death drew nearer she no doubt began to worry about the life of intrigue and sinfulness that she had led. No doubt the bequest to the poor of Upminster was a last-minute attempt to wipe the slate clean, a meagre gesture for a woman who once held the kingdom in her hand.

The
Essex
Miser

Essex is not particularly known for its misers, but it can boast a classic case in John Elwes, the son of a successful Southwark brewer who divided his time between London and Essex, having a house in both.

Excessive care with money seems to have run in the Elwes family. His mother starved herself to death and an uncle was also notoriously mean. Elwes himself travelled backwards and forwards between his two houses on horseback; in his pocket he took his supplies for the journey – a frugal selection of two or three hard-boiled eggs and a crust of bread. His drink was whatever water he could find on the way, and his poor horse never knew what it was to be pampered in the stables of a country inn since Elwes believed it could make do with the grass that grew at the roadside.

However, Elwes was not a miserable character, even though he was miserly. He had a good sense of humour and showed it one day when he went out shooting with a man who was known to be a terrible shot. The two men went into separate fields, and then the other gentleman blasted away at something through the hedge. This something turned out to be Elwes, who received several pieces of shot in the cheeks. The

gentleman rushed up to apologise, but Elwes laughed, saying, 'My dear sir, I congratulate you on improving!'

Elwes would walk miles in the rain to save hiring a cab and then would sit for hours in his wet clothes to save the expense of lighting a fire to dry them. A curious side of his nature was that he was also generous, for he would happily lend money to friends with no real hope of getting it back, yet would risk his

80

life to avoid paying a penny at the turnpike gates which then punctuated the roads of the county.

He only ate meat that was so rotten that the butcher had thrown it out and was so reluctant to spend money on the upkeep of his mansion at Stoke Park that it became un-inhabitable. His wealth came from several properties which he rented in London; if ever one of them was without a tenant, he moved in himself to save waste! This was quite easy to manage, since his entire household effects consisted of two beds, two chairs, one table and an old woman. Thus he could move out at a moment's notice, which made it very hard for his family to keep track of him.

One year Elwes had left Essex and gone back to London where his nephew tried to find him. He heard it said that Elwes had gone to look at a house in Great Marlborough Street. In that district, the nephew found a pot boy who said he had seen an old beggar go into a stable and lock it. The nephew tried the stable door and couldn't open it, so he got a blacksmith to force it down. As they entered they heard cries of distress from upstairs, and found Elwes in agony in bed. He said that he'd been ill for several days but that the old woman had abandoned him in his hour of need. A quick search revealed the body of the old woman downstairs.

Elwes had two children, but of course hadn't married either of their mothers as that would have substantially added to his expenses. He considered education a waste and therefore knew little about running a business or keeping accounts. It was reckoned that when he died various people owed him over £150,000.

He ended his days in the house of one of his sons, since he totally refused to make proper arrangements for having him-self looked after. He often dreamed of robbers at this stage of his life and was inclined to accuse others of stealing his money. One day his son went to Elwes' room and found him sitting up in bed, dressed in his outdoor clothes, with a hat on and his staff in his hand – it was as if he was waiting to go on a journey. He died soon after.

81

Sanctuary
in
Brentwood

❧

I N today's more secular society it is not surprising that the church-origins of a lot of English phrases have been rather forgotten. For example, many Essex churches, centuries ago, had no seats except for a bench against the wall. Only the elderly and infirm were allowed to sit on the bench, hence the phrase 'weakest go to the wall.' Another old phrase is 'sanctuary', meaning that someone is in a safe place. This comes from medieval times, when people in trouble could go to the altar in a church and claim protection.

This story of sanctuary at Brentwood concerns a very important nobleman called Hubert de Burgh. Hubert was a powerful man in the early 1200s and was adviser to King John at the time of Magna Carta. He went on to be 'Justiciar' but was sacked by Henry III in 1232 for opposing Henry's foreign policy.

Like all powerful men, Hubert had his enemies, of whom the most treacherous was the Bishop of Winchester. The Bishop turned King Henry against Hubert, and the nobleman was even accused of dishonesty. It was said that he had tried to steal a talisman from the King – a talisman said to be so wonderful that it rendered its wearer invulnerable. Hubert was also accused of influencing the King by witchcraft.

Hubert was wise enough to know that his enemies were closing in on him, and so he sought refuge at a monastery in Surrey. Henry III ordered the Lord Mayor of London to bring him back dead or alive, which he would have been quite happy to do, as Hubert was not popular with the Londoners. Fortunately for Hubert, the Earl of Chester persuaded the King to drop this plan since it posed a real threat of a riot.

Hubert decided to leave Surrey and join his wife in Bury St Edmunds, and on the way there stopped at the Bishop of Norwich's house in Brentwood. Henry thought that Hubert was trying to leave the country and decided to arrest him. He sent Godfrey de Craumaunde and three hundred men into Essex with instructions to bring Hubert back and put him in the Tower of London.

Hubert had been asleep but fled into the adjacent church as soon as he heard of Godfrey's arrival. In fact Hubert was in such a rush that he didn't have time to collect his clothes, and had to enter the church stark naked. Once inside he went to the altar and took up the cross in one hand and the bread of the body of Christ in the other. Thus he claimed sanctuary and, according to all the accepted traditions of the day, should have been left alone.

However, one of Godfrey's companions was a foreign knight who had no scruples about the sanctuary laws, and he simply rushed in and dragged poor, naked Hubert out. They planned to have him put in chains before taking him to London, but the local blacksmith refused to do the work because of Hubert's reputation for heroic deeds in the past.

Nonetheless Hubert was given some rough treatment and was duly taken to the Tower. Now the Church was not at all pleased about all this, since its privileges had been violated by the King's men. The Bishop of London complained about the invasion of the sanctuary and said that he would excommunicate everyone involved unless Hubert was released. This was a very serious threat in those days, for 'excommunication' meant being cut off from the Church, and to most that implied eternal damnation.

Not surprisingly, Henry gave in to the Bishop's wishes and Hubert was released. He returned to Brentwood, but the Sheriff was ordered to prevent his escape. The church and the Bishop's house in Brentwood were surrounded with trenches and guarded day and night to prevent Hubert's escape. For a while two servants were allowed to take food in each day, but soon even that was stopped.

Hubert knew that sanctuary would keep him safe from the King, but it wouldn't keep him safe from starvation, so eventually he gave himself up and was returned to the Tower once more. In an effort to pacify Henry, Hubert handed over all his riches to the King.

The King allowed Hubert to retire to a castle at Devizes in Wiltshire, where he was under a sort of house-arrest. Even then the Bishop of Winchester was still plotting to have him killed.

There is a happy ending to the story, however. In 1234 the King changed his mind about Hubert and he was restored to all his rights and property. He lived a few more years in comparative peace before dying in 1243. No doubt he always remembered his midnight dash to the church in Brentwood.

The
Courageous Men
of Clacton

THE coast of north-east Essex is famous for its trio of resort towns – Clacton, Frinton and Walton. Each is known for its dry climate and the gentle east coast breezes that give the air a freshness that many other resorts seem to lack. But those gentle breezes have a habit of turning into autumn gales as soon as visitors have left, and the friendly sea can become a dangerous enemy.

So it is that Clacton is also famous for the exploits of its first lifeboat, the *Albert Edward*. This was first stationed in the town in 1878, but it wasn't until 1881 that the little boat became famous for its heroic deeds.

The last ten days of October that year were marked by howling gales across the country. In Clacton, trees were uprooted and chimneys blown down. On Friday evening, when most people were glad that the week's work was over so that they could huddle indoors, distress signals were seen out to sea in the direction of the Maplin Light.

The crew of the *Albert Edward* didn't pause to worry about the weather, but set off into the stormy sea as quickly as they could at about 8 pm. They had a distinguished visitor on board – the Lifeboat Inspector for the district, who happened to be staying in the town.

After a perilous journey the *Albert Edward* discovered the schooner *Ocean* caught on the Maplin Sands and leaking badly. It was on its way from Hartlepool with a crew of five and a cargo of firebricks, but had been blown onto the dangerous sands. Water was filling the poor *Ocean* and its small crew were exhausted after hours of frantic pumping.

The fresher men from the lifeboat took over the pumping until extra help in the shape of a tug from Gravesend arrived. The tug hitched a line to the two other vessels and then towed them both to Poplar in the river Thames, the Clacton men pumping away in the *Ocean* all the while. At Poplar quite a crowd of people turned out to greet the heroes, one of whom was a policeman. This was very fortunate, since a crewman from the *Ocean* tried to steal away with a lifeboatman's coat and was caught by the vigilant officer; one month in prison was the penalty. Some people are never grateful!

The *Albert Edward* was then towed back to Clacton by the steamer *Glen Loch*; its epic voyage had kept it away from home for 44 hours.

Only nine days after setting out to save the *Ocean*, the *Albert Edward* was back in action again.

This time the vessel in peril was the *Madeline*, a brand new fishing boat from Boulogne. It had been busy catching herrings and had 19 tons of fish on board packed into barrels, together with 100 barrels of salt and 300 empty barrels. At 6.30 pm on Saturday evening the *Madeline* was blown onto Gunfleet Sands with heavy rain all around. Sixteen Frenchmen stood to lose their lives, so distress signals were fired off straight away. Unfortunately the rain was so heavy that no-one on the Essex coast saw these signals until the coastguard at Clacton spotted them at dawn on the Sunday.

The men of the *Albert Edward* were called into action immediately, but coxswain Robert Legerton faced a serious problem. The wind was blowing from the south-east and this would make it very difficult to sail the lifeboat out from its normal starting point; its only power came from sails and oars, insufficient to take it headlong into the gale.

Thinking quickly, Legerton had the lifeboat taken down to the West Swin from where he hoped to get a steamer to tow it out to sea. The first ship he hailed ignored his desperate request, but the *Contest* proved to have a more helpful captain. Not only did the captain agree to the towing idea, but he also provided the lifeboat crew with a bucket of biscuits, beef, bread and cherry brandy!

There can be no doubt that Legerton's quick thinking saved the French crew from certain death, because by the time the Clacton men reached the sands they found the *Madeline* keeled over with its men huddled in one corner out of the water. Even as they arrived the sea was breaking over the wreck, whose captain later said that another half hour on the sands and it would have broken up completely, with the crew being drowned.

As the *Albert Edward* approached a heavy surge threw the French boat further up the sands away from rescue. As the *Albert Edward* made a second approach there was another surge, this time smashing the lifeboat into the fishing boat and damaging its rudder.

Clearly Legerton would lose his own crew if he attempted to get too close again, so he began to pull in the Frenchmen by lines. A boy was rescued using a boat hook whilst one man was saved through clinging to the beard of Clacton man John Greer. Greer later described this experience as 'not at all pleasant' – which must have been an understatement!

The exhausted lifeboatmen returned as heroes to Clacton, with the story of the rescue appearing in newspapers across Britain and France. The French Government even awarded medals to the crew.

BEFORE   AFTER

The
Billericay
Diet

THESE days there seem to be any number of 'recommended' ways of losing weight. Most people have heard of going jogging or of doing aerobics. For the more dedicated slimmers there are many diets to choose from. But how many Essex people have ever heard of the spectacular effects of the Billericay Diet?

The 'inventor' of this strange diet – it actually cut out *all* drink – was an overweight miller from Billericay called Thomas Wood. He was born on 30th November 1719 and clearly belonged to a tolerably well-off family since his parents were known for their 'intemperate mode of living' – in other words, they ate and drank far too much.

Thomas, probably because he took after his parents, was an unhealthy child. After his parents died he took over the running of the family windmill and was successful enough to build a second. For a time he used to organise firework displays at a spot halfway between the two mills.

Wood also continued the family tradition of eating excessively. It was his habit to have large meals of fatty meat three times a day, interspersed with huge quantities of butter, cheese and ale. For a while he suffered no effects from this vast amount of food, and was said to be so strong that he could lift two huge flour sacks on his own.

The large meals didn't have any effect on Wood until he reached the age of about forty. Then he became 'stout' and suffered a whole variety of medical problems. His sleep was disturbed, he had a constant thirst, after meals he often had a feeling of suffocation, he suffered fits of depression and was attacked regularly by epilepsy, rheumatism and gout. In short he was a physical wreck, and an enormously fat one too.

He was not a lazy man, however, for he worked hard at his business, kept bees with great success, and was such a friend to the birds that apparently they would eat out of his hand. However his physical problems began to cause him depression, until by 1764 he was in a terrible state.

It was at this point that a local clergyman lent Wood a copy of an unusual book. This was *Discourses on a Sober and Temperate Life* by Cornaro. Wood read the book avidly, and it changed his life (in contrast to the many books which today's publishers advertise with the phrase, 'This book will change your life', which usually have no effect whatsoever!). Wood decided immediately to begin the gradual reform of his diet. The first step he made was to reduce his consumption of animal foods and to limit his ale to one pint a day.

Encouraged by the results of this initial step, the miller reduced his meat consumption still further and limited ale to only half a pint a day. On 4th January 1765 he stopped drinking malt liquors altogether. Over the next few months he ceased eating meat, butter, and cheese altogether as well, and then – on 25th October – took his most remarkable step of all when he stopped drinking anything at all. Not even water passed his lips, only the occasional drop of medicine, although on 9th May 1766 he did relent slightly by taking $2\frac{1}{2}$ glasses of water – but it is believed that he never touched another drop after that.

He used dumb-bells to exercise himself, made long walks every morning, and took cold baths twice a week – this was then seen as a medical treatment for extreme cases only!

For a little while he lived on nothing but sea biscuits, but seems to have lived most of his last twenty years on nothing but dumplings, which must have been very cheap since he made the flour himself! Every morning he would boil 1lb of flour in 1½ pints of milk, and this formed his entire sustenance for the day. It was even said that he carried the flour for his dumplings around in his pockets, especially when he travelled to market at Romford; this seems a little unlikely – the flour in his pockets was probably taken to Romford as 'samples' to show customers.

Wood also changed his sleeping pattern, going to bed at 8 pm and rising at 1 am or 2 am every morning. This appeared to have done him no harm at all. His strength returned and he was able to lift ¼ ton unaided – more than he could manage at the age of thirty.

In his own words, Wood changed from 'a monster to a person of moderate size; from the condition of an unhealthy decrepit old man, to perfect health'. This transformation attracted medical attention and a certain Doctor Baker examined him. Baker found that Wood had lost about eleven stones without any apparent harm; he could not be more certain about the weight since Wood shared a common superstition about being weighed. His pulse was much lower than normal, registering only 45 even after a six-hour walk. His abstinence from any drink also excited the doctor's attention.

Baker was most interested in Wood's healthy appearance. His flesh was firm and his complexion good. Nor did his stomach betray the effects of a hasty diet:

'. . . the integuments of his belly, which I expected to have found loose and pendulous, are contracted nearly in proportion to his diminished bulk.'

In other words – no loose folds of flesh!

Wood became happy and healthy, even his bad dreams came to an end. As far as is known he continued on his diet for many years – he was certainly still on it in 1775 – and he died on 21st May 1783.

So one answer for those who worry about their figure is

simple – try the Billericay Diet and live off dumplings alone. At least it will prove a lot cheaper than modern 'health food' diets!

An
Essex
Martyr

T HE early morning air was still damp and heavy from the
overnight rain as Sheriff Brocket arrived at the *Swan Inn*,
Brentwood, to begin his gloomy task. Heavy clouds covered
the sky, threatening more rain as the day progressed. Brocket
had arrived to organise the burning of one of the men imprisoned at the *Swan*. The one he had come for was William
Hunter, a nineteen-year-old apprentice to a London silk-
weaver, sentenced to death in Queen Mary's England for his
refusal to turn from his Protestant faith.

Hunter was one of many Essex men and women executed
for their Protestant faith at this time. The faith was particularly strong in the county since it had spread across the North
Sea from Germany, entering Essex through its many trading
links with the continent.

At least twenty-three were burned at Colchester, including
six in one fire. Seventeen Essex men and women were taken to
Smithfield for burning, five of them coming from Bocking.
Twelve more were burnt at Stratford and four others taken to
Islington. In 1555 the policy seems to have been to spread the
burnings around the county, so that people were burnt at
Horndon, Rayleigh, Braintree, Maldon and several other
places.

The way by which William Hunter became a martyr at Brentwood on 26th March 1555 was a long and arduous one. He had been an apprentice in London, but the pressure to attend Catholic Mass one Easter caused him to return to his parents in Brentwood.

A few weeks later he visited a chapel nearby and was reading the Bible when disturbed by another man. This man disliked the trend of Hunter's argument and fetched the local Catholic priest – who was apparently in the alehouse next door!

The priest and Hunter had a fierce argument over the meaning of some verses from the Gospel of John, chapter VI. The result of this was that the priest called Hunter a heretic. Hunter, in his youthful enthusiasm, seems to have rather goaded and antagonised the priest – 'I would that you and I were even now fast tied to a stake, to prove whether that you or I would stand strongest to our faith,' he cried. The result of this outburst was that the constable was sent for and William fled, but he later gave himself up on account of his fears for his father.

A succession of people tried to change Hunter's mind. He was interviewed at length by Bonner, the Bishop of London, who was much impressed by the young Essex man. The Bishop tried to get Hunter to confess secretly, but he refused even this chance to escape the stake.

He was then placed in the stocks at the Bishop's gatehouse, with only a cup of water and a crust of bread to sustain him. He touched neither of these, maintaining a fast for two days until he was removed for further questioning by the Bishop. However, Hunter turned down all Bonner's pleas, and so was placed in the dungeons in irons.

Five or six times the Bishop interviewed him, and every time Hunter gave the same answers. He was even offered £40 and the freedom of London if he would recant; he would not. Eventually the Bishop's patience wore thin and, after a month in Newgate, Hunter was sent back to Brentwood to be executed as a warning to all like-minded people.

94

There he met his parents again, and they offered him their support. Whilst he was imprisoned at the *Swan* with other Protestants, they visited him. William spoke tenderly to his mother, telling her that 'for my little pain which I shall suffer, which is but a short braide, Christ hath promised me a crown of joy'.

Sheriff Brocket arrived with soldiers and guards to execute the heretic, not so much because he feared an escape attempt but because there were many who held Protestant views in the district and so trouble was a possibility. Even the Sheriff's own household was divided, for as Hunter stepped forward Brocket's son grasped hold of him and offered encouragement. A few confused words tumbled out, then the young Brocket was made speechless by his sobs.

Hunter stepped out into the morning air, meeting his father along the way to the place of execution. 'God be with you, son William', the father said, and William assured him that they would meet again in happier times. Added poignancy was given to this meeting through the fact that William had given himself up in order to save his family from persecution.

When William arrived at the execution place he found that everything was still unready – just as he had dreamed they would be. He even had time to kneel down on the wet faggots of wood to recite a psalm.

Hunter's prayers were interrupted by a Catholic who claimed he was misusing the words, and then by the reading out of an offer of pardon from Queen Mary if he would recant. With no hesitation, Hunter rejected this offer, then walked over to the stake and stood there patiently whilst a chain was fastened around him.

An argumentative by-stander named Brown complained about the arrangements. 'There is not enough wood to burn a leg of him', he moaned, and when Hunter asked for prayers, Brown told him that he would rather pray for his dog.

Hunter turned his face up towards the heavy grey clouds that covered the sky. 'Son of God shine upon me', he called out. Suddenly the sun burst through, shining so brightly into his face that the young man had to look down. Was the dramatic appearance of the sun on such a dismal morning a miracle? The people were left to wonder.

As the fire was lit the crowd muttered in sympathy. 'I pray God have mercy on his soul', one man cried out, supported by calls of 'Amen' from several others.

Then Hunter threw his Psalm Book to his watching brother, called out, 'Lord receive my spirit', and was lost from sight amidst the smoke and flames.